AF227694

This book is dedicated to my children:

Adoniah, Jeremiah, Kaya, and David

I wouldn't be a super mama without you !

To my dear friend I appreciate your words of encouragement and telling me I am a super mama!

You are a Super Mama, you are so tough!

You rise to the occasion even when you had enough.

You are a Super Mama. You are undefeated.

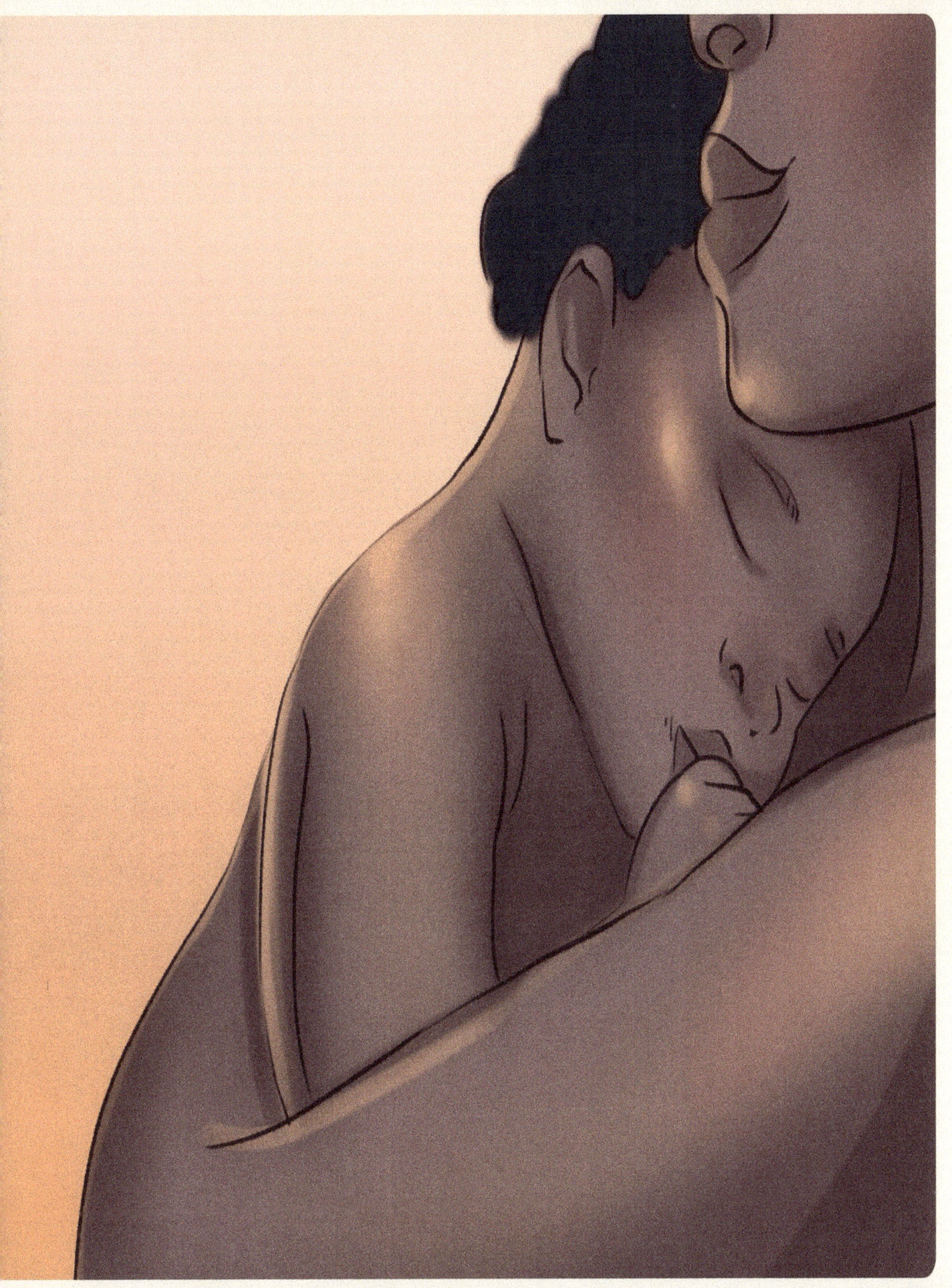

Your house is clean, and your kids are never mistreated.

You are a Super Mama no matter the cost, whether single, married, in a partnership or divorced.

Whether doing it on your own, you overcome obstacles.

Hold you head high and never look back.

Continue striving towards the moon.

And reaching for the stars.

Because you're a Super Mama wherever you

are.

A Note for ALL MOMS

The world goes around because of you, thank you for all that you do.

And thank you do, and thank you for our mothers, godmothers, grandmothers, partners and friends that have paved the way for us to become great moms.

Thank you to Fathers, grandfathers, godfathers, pastors and community leaders.

Strive to be the best mom you can be and do the best job you can do.

If you need help there are organizations that can assist you in your respective community, and it is okay to get help if you need it.

Keep your head up!

I love you,

Crystal DeBouse

About the Author

Crystal De Bouse is Brooklyn, New York Native. She moved to Albany, New York in 2011, after serving 8 years overseas in Japan and Germany, with the United States Air Force.

She completed her Master of Science Degree in Early Childhood Education in 2015 from: The College of Saint Rose. She is a mother of four, her children: Adoniah (9), Jeremiah (8), Kaya (6), and David (4) are her inspiration and motivation. In her free time, she loves to travel. Crystal is also a model, singer and songwriter, and manages her rental property and Airbnb: The Urban G3M.

For all inquiries email: crystaldebouse@gmail.com.